BUILDING RESILIENCE

Growing Friendships

HONOR HEAD

CRABTREE
PUBLISHING COMPANY
WWW.CRABTREEBOOKS.COM

CRABTREE
PUBLISHING COMPANY
WWW.CRABTREEBOOKS.COM

Published in Canada
Crabtree Publishing
616 Welland Ave.
St. Catharines, Ontario
L2M 5V6

Published in the United States
Crabtree Publishing
347 Fifth Avenue
Suite 1402–145
New York, NY 10016

Published in 2021 by Crabtree Publishing Company

First published in Great Britain in 2020
by The Watts Publishing Group
Copyright © The Watts Publishing Group, 2020

Author: Honor Head

Editorial director: Kathy Middleton

Editors: Amy Pimperton, Ellen Rodger

Proofreader: Melissa Boyce

Designers: Peter Scoulding and Cathryn Gilbert

Cover design: Peter Scoulding

**Production coordinator
and Prepress technician:** Tammy McGarr

Print coordinator: Katherine Berti

Consultant: Clare Arnold, psychotherapist and child and adolescent mental health services professional

Printed in the U.S.A./012021/CG20201102

Picture credits
Shutterstock: Kurit Afshen 27t, 28l; andamanec 22b; AndreAnita 15t; ArCalu 23r; Agnieszka Bacal 17c; Natalia Bachkova 2, 14, 30c; Masha Basova 27b; Henk Bentlage 4; Uwe Bergwitz 6; un.bolovan 21b; Ryan M Bolton 25cl; borgil 29t; Ekaterina Brusnika 11b; Ken Calderhead 19b; Abhay Chaware 19t; Phuwadon Chulasukhont 29cr; Belle Ciezak 23l, 32; Danita Delmont 26; dezy 7cl, 15bl, 30t; Celso Diniz 7tr; Alexander Ermolaev front cover; fontoknak 15cr; gadag 5cl, 30b; Giedrius 11c; Joe Gough 9bc; Pascale Gueret 7br; Miroslav Halama 20; hiopex 13b; Eric isselee 13t; Ammit Jack 5tr; Kletr 18; knelson 19c; Grigorita Ko 8c; Panagiotis Komninelis 25r; Steve Lagreca 12; Rich Lindie 24b; Lubava 17t; Natalia Lukiyanova 11t; marima 9tr; Katho Menden 16; MizKitty 21c; Nagel Photography 9l; Kelly Nelson 28-29b; Noheapphotos 27c; panda3800 22t; PIPPO-CHI 17b; Ondrej Prosicky 5br, 21t; Villiers Steyn 24t; Tap10 13c; Dwi Yulianto 10.

Library and Achives Canada Cataloguing in Publication

Title: Growing friendships / Honor Head.
Other titles: Friendships and bullying
Names: Head, Honor, author.
Description: Series statement: Building resilience | Previously published under title: Friendships and bullying. | Includes index.
Identifiers: Canadiana (print) 20200357085 | Canadiana (ebook) 20200357174
 ISBN 9781427128218 (hardcover) |
 ISBN 9781427128256 (softcover) |
 ISBN 9781427128294 (HTML)
Subjects: LCSH: Friendship—Juvenile literature. | LCSH: Friendship— Psychological aspects—Juvenile literature.
Classification: LCC BF575.F66 H43 2021 | DDC j158.2/5—dc23

Library of Congress Cataloging-in-Publication Data

Names: Head, Honor, author.
Title: Growing friendships / Honor Head.
Description: New York, NY : Crabtree Publishing Company, 2021. | Series: Building resilience | Includes index.
Identifiers: LCCN 2020045185 (print) | LCCN 2020045186 (ebook) |
 ISBN 9781427128218 (hardcover) |
 ISBN 9781427128256 (paperback) |
 ISBN 9781427128294 (ebook)
Subjects: LCSH: Friendship in children--Juvenile literature. | Friendship-- Juvenile literature.
Classification: LCC BF723.F68 H43 2021 (print) | LCC BF723.F68 (ebook) | DDC 177/.62--dc23
LC record available at https://lccn.loc.gov/2020045185
LC ebook record available at https://lccn.loc.gov/2020045186

Contents

Everyone faces challenging times in their life. This book will help you to develop the resilience skills you need to cope with difficult situations in all areas of life.

What does it mean to build resilience?

When we build resilience we can better cope with things, such as being bullied or losing a friend. Building resilience means we accept that times are difficult now, but that we can and will get back to enjoying life. Learning how to build resilience is a valuable life skill.

What is a trusted adult?

A trusted adult is anyone that you trust and who makes you feel safe. It can be a parent or caregiver, a relative, or a teacher. If you have no one you want to talk to, phone a helpline (see page 32).

What is friendship?

Friendship is about sharing. Not just sharing things, but sharing your time and your feelings. When you share, you make people feel special and cared for. Sharing also makes you feel good about yourself.

Sharing is fun and makes everyone feel happy.

When you have resilience, or inner strength, you can bounce back when sad things happen. Feeling good about yourself and having friends who care about you can help you to be resilient.

A special friend is someone that you can turn to. Having a friend that you can **trust** helps your **self-confidence**. Friends can help you to build up your resilience. This makes it easier for you to cope at sad or difficult times.

Someone who bullies you, shouts at you, or is rude or mean to you is not a good friend. A true friend cares about how they make you feel.

Everyone needs friends

Finding a good friend is very special. Friends are people you enjoy being with. They make you feel happy. Friends help you through the bad times and are with you to enjoy the good times.

Friends can be like you or be completely different.

Friends cheer you up when you feel sad. They are there to give you a hug, hold your hand, or just listen. A real friend is someone who tries to understand how you feel.

Being with friends can be exciting and fun. Just spending quiet time together can feel special too. Friends help to make happy memories you will have forever. Happy memories help you to bounce back when you are going through difficult times.

A true friend never laughs at you or makes you feel silly. Good friends always say sorry if they upset you.

Making new friends

Take a deep breath and look forward to meeting new people.

You will meet new people and make new friends all your life. Making friends can be a bit scary, but remember, everyone feels **nervous** meeting new people. Smile and be polite and friendly. Most people will behave the same way to you.

Talk to a trusted adult if you feel **anxious** about meeting new people. We are all different in many ways, but nearly everyone wants to be liked and loved.

Many people feel shy about meeting others. Look for someone who is standing alone or being quiet. Smile and say "hello." They probably feel shy too. Feeling shy is OK.

Asking questions shows that you want to be friends. Make sure you listen to the answer without interrupting.

Being unfriendly

Not everyone will want to be friendly and there is nothing you can do about this. If some people don't want to be friends, think good thoughts, and try again with other people.

Remember, if someone does not want to be your friend, it is not because of you.

You do not have to change who you are to make friends. Be proud of who you are and be yourself. Accept others for the way they are too.

If others ignore you, whisper behind your back, or leave you out of things, this might be a form of bullying. Tell a trusted adult if you feel you are being bullied. Try not to let what other people say upset you.

Some people like to have a lot of friends. Some like to have one or two best friends. How many friends you have is not important. What is important is to have friends you can trust and who make you feel safe and loved.

What kind of friend are you?

Are you kind and helpful or **bossy** and mean?
Do you listen or do you only think about what you want
to say? Are you happy when your friends have good
luck or do something well, or do you feel **jealous**?

There are many ways to make sure you are a good friend.

Think of ways to help and support your friends. Let your friends know you are there to listen to them. Be there to help them work through any problems.

Be happy for your friends when something good happens to them. There is no reason to feel jealous. When your turn comes, it will be great to have friends who feel happy for you.

Take a deep breath before you say something that might upset someone. Think about how you would feel if someone said the same thing to you.

If you feel angry or jealous, talk to a trusted adult about it. Don't let these feelings grow and get worse. They might make you say or do nasty or mean things.

Friendships take work

To make a friendship work, we need trust, **loyalty**, **respect**, and **forgiveness**. We need to understand how other people feel. This is called empathy.

We trust friends and feel safe with them.

Friends don't have to agree about everything. Even close friends can have disagreements. It's important to respect what other people think and say as long as what they say is not hurting anyone.

If you have an argument with a friend and it is your fault, say sorry.

If your friend has upset you, try not to shout or get angry. Maybe there is a good reason for what happened. Talk about it to understand the problem and be friends again.

Enjoy sharing

Sharing with other people makes you feel good about yourself. Learning how to share and take turns can be difficult. It can be hard to give something to someone else when you want to keep it.

Sharing helps us to play and work together as a team.

If your friend wants to share something, such as a toy, talk about a fair way to share it. You could agree to take turns where each of you has the toy for 10 minutes.

While you are waiting for your turn, think about other things you can do. You might find something more interesting to do. Sometimes, we only want something because someone else has it, not because we really want it.

If your best friend spends time with another person, it may make you feel jealous, hurt, or angry. But think! If your friend likes someone else, you might like them too. Maybe you can all be friends.

Be kind

Being kind is when you do or say things to help others. Doing something kind makes people feel good. It makes people smile. Try to be kind to everyone, not just your friends.

Being kind to others helps you to feel good about yourself.

When you feel angry or that something is unfair, you might say something mean rather than explaining how you feel. If this happens, talk to your friend about why you feel this way.

If you do get angry or upset, think of something else. Bounce back by singing your favorite song. You could walk away or have a drink of water until the feeling passes.

If someone is unkind to you, it is OK to feel angry or sad. It is also OK to cry. Crying is a natural way to let out your feelings. You are not "acting like a baby" if you cry. You are letting it out so you can feel better.

Stand up for yourself

If you have a friend who is very bossy or doesn't know how to share, don't get angry. Talk to your friend and say that you are not happy with what is going on.

Sometimes, bossy people don't want to listen to others.

Talk to a trusted adult about what to say to your friend. Try **role-playing** the scene. Your adult can pretend to be your friend.

Take a deep breath and tell your friend how you feel. Don't shout or be rude. If your friend will not listen, walk away and try again another time.

If your friends say you are bossy, don't get angry or say you are not bossy. Think about your behavior. Talk to a grown-up you trust about it. Maybe you are bossy and you don't realize it.

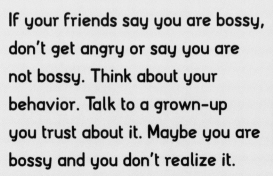

Friendships change

Sometimes a good friend may not want to be best friends anymore. Or you may meet another person you want to be friends with. This is OK. Some friendships will last for a very long time and others will not.

When a friendship ends, you may think that you did something wrong. Unless your friend has said you did something to upset them, do not blame yourself for what has happened.

Accepting that friendships end can help you bounce back when they do.

If you lose a friend you may feel lonely and angry. It is OK to feel sad and cry. Talk about how you feel or write down your feelings. The bad feeling will pass.

As you grow up, sometimes friends grow apart and want to do different things. Losing a friend happens to everyone. Talk to your family about it. They can help you feel better.

Bullying

Some people are bullies. They don't like to share, are rude, and say mean things. Some bullies hurt people by hitting, pushing, or pulling hair. Others use mean words to make you fear them.

Stay away from people that bully you or upset you.

If you are being bullied, it is not your fault. No one deserves to be bullied. Keep away from the bully if you can. Try not to be mean back to them.

Talk to an adult you trust about anyone who is bullying you. You do not have to put up with being bullied.

Are you a bully? Think about why you bully others. Build resilience by talking to someone about your behavior and how you can change it. People are there to support you and help you to understand why you bully others.

Making friends online

Sometimes friends connect with friends or make new friends on the Internet. Making **digital** friends is different from real-life friends because you cannot see the people you are talking to.

Being online is fun and exciting, but you have to be careful.

You can strengthen real-life friendships online. Making new friends online is trickier. It is easy for people to pretend to be kind and friendly online. It is important to be careful. Your parents or caregivers should know about your online friends. Do not share information such as your full name or address.

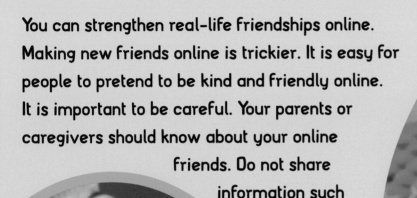

Some people may lie about who they are or ask you to keep secrets. They might say things that upset and frighten you. If this happens, turn off the device and tell a trusted adult right away.

Don't forget your real-life friends. Never arrange to meet a digital friend or stranger offline.

Online bullying

Online bullying is called cyberbullying. Even if you are not active with friends online now, you may be in the future. You may find not everyone online will be nice. Some people may be nasty and rude. Ignore these people.

Find sites online that make you feel happy.

People online often say mean things because they do not have to face the person they are bullying. Bounce back by remembering that you have real friends and family who care about you.

On some sites, you may post pictures that others can "like." Remember, you don't need online likes to feel good about yourself. If you like the picture you posted, that is all that matters.

If people say nasty things about anything you post online, just get offline. Read a book, listen to music, or plan to meet real-life friends.

Be resilient!

Being resilient means being able to cope with times when you feel sad or are going through a situation that makes you feel afraid or anxious. Here is a reminder of how friendships are a great way to help you become resilient.

- Friends can make you feel cared for and supported. They can help build your self-confidence.

- Having the support of friends gives you the confidence to try new things, explore, and be adventurous.

- Having friends that come to you for support when they feel sad or upset makes you feel worthwhile. Hugging a sad friend makes you feel good and helps your friend.

- We have to learn to accept it when friends don't want to be friendly any more. We learn that this is not our fault and find new friends. This will help you to bounce back from feeling sad.

- It is important to learn the difference between good and bad friends. Bad friends are bullies and make us feel small and unhappy. We should still be kind to mean people, but not allow them to hurt us.

Notes for parents, caregivers, and teachers

There are many ways parents, caregivers, and teachers can help children develop resilience skills through friendships.

Encourage children to be adventurous and to experiment and try new things. Reinforce that failure is not a bad thing, but can be very positive. Having fun and trying new things is more important than doing it right.

By trying new things, children are more likely to meet a wide range of people, which will increase their social skills and build a network of friends.

Talk to children about friendships and what friends mean to them. Discuss how they treat friends and how they expect friends to treat them.

Talk about the differences between good and bad friendships. Discuss how their behavior affects others and vice versa.

Role-play different friendship scenarios: fighting, being mean, refusing to share, losing a friend. How does it make them feel? Discuss ways to cope with negative feelings.

Discuss with children the ways that they can control a friendship: by being kind, thoughtful, and helpful, and not allowing others to bully them. Discuss the ways that they cannot control a friendship, for example, a friend choosing other friends to be with or not sharing. Having control builds confidence. Learning and accepting that we cannot control other people builds resilience.

Read through this book. Talk about the topics on each page. Role-play a situation relating to the topic.

Finally, not all children will have or want lots of friends. Some may just have one or two special friends. Some children prefer to spend time by themselves. All children are different, so don't force friendships on a child. However, if you feel your child is being antisocial or seems to be isolated from others, talk to the child and see if there is an underlying reason, such as bullying or excessive anxiety. Don't feel ashamed to talk to a doctor or teacher about the situation if you think this will help.

Glossary

anxious Feeling worried or nervous about how something is going to turn out

bossy Someone who likes to tell others what to do

digital Something computer-related

forgiveness To stop being angry with someone for something that they did

jealous Being angry or upset if someone has something you want

loyalty Helping and supporting someone

nervous Feeling scared or worried about something

respect To understand how another person feels

role-playing To act out a situation by pretending to be the people involved

self-confidence Believing you are good enough to do things well

trust To believe that someone is reliable and truthful

Websites and helplines

If you need advice or someone to talk to, visit these websites or try these helplines.

www.boystown.org is an organization that helps children and youth in the United States. It has a helpline that has trained English and Spanish counselors working 24 hours a day, every day of the year. Call 1-800-448-3000.

www.kidshelpphone.ca has helpful information for children and youth in Canada. It has a helpline with trained English and French counselors. Call 1-800-668-6868.

www.mindyourmind.ca is a helpful website that gives tips on coping with issues and how to ask people for help.

Index